JumpStart Your Leadership

Books by Dr. John C. Maxwell
Can Teach You How to Be a REAL Success

Relationships

25 Ways to Win with People

Becoming a Person of Influence

Encouragement Changes Everything

Ethics 101

Everyone Communicates,
Few Connect

The Power of Partnership

Relationships 101

Winning With People

Equipping

The 15 Invaluable Laws of Growth

The 17 Essential Qualities
of a Team Player

The 17 Indisputable Laws
of Teamwork

Developing the Leaders Around You

Equipping 101

Make Today Count

Mentoring 101

My Dream Map

Partners in Prayer

Put Your Dream to the Test

Running with the Giants

Talent Is Never Enough

Today Matters

Your Road Map for Success

Attitude

Attitude 101

The Difference Maker

Failing Forward

How Successful People Think

Sometimes You Win,
Sometimes You Learn

Success 101

Thinking for a Change

The Winning Attitude

Leadership

The 10th Anniversary Edition
of The 21 Irrefutable Laws
of Leadership

The 21 Indispensable Qualities
of a Leader

The 21 Most Powerful Minutes
in a Leader's Day

The 360 Degree Leader

Developing the Leader Within You

The 5 Levels of Leadership

Go for Gold

How Successful People Lead

Leadership 101

Leadership Gold

Leadership Promises for
Every Day

A 90-DAY
IMPROVEMENT
PLAN

JumpStart Your Leadership

JOHN C. MAXWELL

CENTER
STREET

NEW YORK   BOSTON   NASHVILLE

The author is represented by Yates & Yates, LLP,
Literary Agency, Orange, California.

Literary development and design: Koechel Peterson & Associates, Inc.,
Minneapolis, Minnesota.

This book has been adapted from *The 5 Levels of Leadership*, copyright ©
2011 by John C. Maxwell. Published by Center Street.

Center Street
Hachette Book Group
1290 Avenue of the Americas
New York, NY 10104

www.CenterStreet.com

Printed in the United States of America

RRD-C

First trade edition: December 2014
10 9 8 7 6 5 4 3 2 1

Center Street is a division of Hachette Book Group, Inc.
The Center Street name and logo are trademarks of Hachette Book Group,
Inc.

The Hachette Speakers Bureau provides a wide range of authors for speaking events. To find out more, go to www.hachettespeakersbureau.com or call
(866) 376-6591.

The publisher is not responsible for websites (or their content) that are not
owned by the publisher.

ISBN 978-1-4555-6112-4

JUMPSTART YOUR LEADERSHIP

*I*NTRODUCTION

*S*o you want to jumpstart your leadership. Perhaps you are an experienced leader who wants to fine-tune your leadership skills. Or you are facing challenges as a leader that you're having a difficult time solving. Or you're new to the workplace and aspire to make a difference by increasing your influence. All of those are worthy goals.

Regardless of your reason for wanting to improve, I am very excited to present you with this 90-day plan to better your leadership. Why? Because everything rises and falls on leadership. If you want to make a positive impact on the world, learning to lead better will help you do it.

Leadership is one of my passions. I've been on a leadership journey for 50 years and have dedicated my life to sharing with others what I am learning about leading.

I began the journey by asking many of the questions you probably have been asking yourself:

What is a leader?

How should I define leadership?

Where does leadership start?

What should I do first?

How can I increase my influence with others?

How can I develop a productive team?

How can I keep getting better as a leader?

Sometimes leadership questions can be difficult to answer. But leadership does not have to be confusing or overwhelming. In fact, anyone can learn to become a better leader. Why do I say that? Because *leadership is influence*. If you can increase your influence with others, you can lead more effectively.

Too often people associate leadership advancement with their career path. That's the wrong paradigm. What you should be thinking about is your own leadership development! The sign of good leadership isn't personal advancement. It's the advancement of your team. When others succeed and your team gets better, it's a sign that your leadership is improving.

Over the next 90 days, you will be provided with clear steps to help you develop in key areas of leadership. You'll be reminded to take your focus off of a job title and explore how to earn the respect and trust of your team by developing relationships. As you do, people will want to follow you. From there we'll give more attention to how to develop the team and increase their productivity. Finally, we'll focus on how you can share what you've learned to help the people you lead to become leaders in their own right.

No matter where you are in your leadership or what challenges you face, you have a choice to improve your leadership from this day forward. You can become a better leader! To do that, all I ask is that is you consistently set aside 15 minutes every day for the next 90 days to improve your leadership. Think about the inspirational quote, read the brief lesson, reflect on the included question, and move forward by writing a response or taking action.

If you don't have a leadership position yet, realize that adopting these same principles into your life now will open the leadership door in the future.

Ready? Let's get started!

DAY

1

The secret of success in life is for a man to be ready for his opportunity when it comes.

BENJAMIN DISRAELI

Most of the time when a person first enters into leadership, it means that the person in authority believes that the new leader has some degree of potential for leading. That's good news. So if you're being invited to lead something, then celebrate the fact that someone in authority believes in you, and let me say welcome to the first tangible step in your leadership journey. You have a seat at the table and will have opportunities to express your opinion and make decisions. Your initial goal should be to show your leader and your team that you deserve the responsibility you have received.

Who has given you opportunities to lead? What qualities do you possess that you think influenced that decision?

DAY

2

Destiny is no matter of chance.
It is a matter of choice.
It is not a thing to be waited for;
it is a thing to be achieved.

WILLIAM JENNINGS BRYAN

Becoming a leader isn't a mystical subject. It can be approached very practically, and everyone has the potential to become a better leader. So what is your leadership potential? Do you have the capacity and the desire to become a good leader, even a great leader? There's only one way to find out. Accept the leadership challenge before you now, give growth your best effort, and dive into leadership. If you're willing to pick up the gauntlet, you'll never regret it, because there is no better way to increase your positive impact on the world and add value to others than to increase your leadership ability.

Think about the people you consider to be great leaders. What qualities do they possess that makes them successful? What do you admire about them as leaders? Do you think you could cultivate those qualities yourself?

DAY

3

*No man is a leader until his appointment is ratified
in the minds and the hearts of his men.*

INFANTRYMAN'S JOURNAL (1954)

Whenever an individual receives leadership responsibility, some level of authority or power usually comes with it. Often in the beginning that power is very limited, but that's okay because most leaders need to prove themselves with little before being given much. If you are a leader, you must learn to use the authority you are given wisely, to advance the team and help the people you lead. Do that, and your people will begin to give you even greater authority. When that happens, you gain leadership, not just a position.

Thinking about the individuals you influence, write down one thing that you are able to do to advance the team that they do not have the ability to do for themselves.

DAY

4

*Before you are a leader, success is all about
growing yourself. When you become a leader,
success is all about growing others.*

JACK WELCH

The journey into leadership will only be successful if you dedicate yourself to continual development. To become an effective leader, you must believe that the leadership position you receive does not make you a leader; rather, it is merely an invitation to grow. Make the most of whatever opportunity in leadership you receive by making growth your goal. If you do that and become a lifetime learner, you will continually increase your influence over time. And you will make the most of your leadership potential, no matter how great or small it might be. Always strive to keep improving.

Make a list of the areas you feel are your strengths. Put a star next to the area where you shine most. How can you develop that area?

DAY

5

Leadership is much less about what you do,
and much more about who you are.

Frances Hesselbein

If you are new to leadership—or new to a particular leadership position—it is the perfect time to think about the leadership style you desire to develop. Your leadership page is blank and you get to fill it in any way you want! What kind of leader do you want to be? Don't just become reactive and develop a style by default. Really think about it. Do you want to be a team builder? Do you want to lift people up? Do you want to be the type of leader who asks questions before giving directions? The choices you make will determine your style. Choose to be your best and bring out the best in others.

Whether you are new to leadership or an experienced leader, describe how you desire to lead. What kind of leader do you have the potential to become?

DAY

6

Hard experience has taught me that real leadership is about understanding yourself first, then using that to create a superb organization.

CAPTAIN MIKE ABRASHOFF

Good leadership begins with leaders knowing who they are. Successful leaders know their own strengths and weaknesses. They understand their temperament. They know what personal experiences serve them well. As a result, they have developed successful work habits and understand their daily, monthly, and seasonal rhythms. They have a sense of where they are going and how they want to get there. They don't pretend to be something they're not. Instead they admit their shortcomings and harness their strengths. As a result, they know what they're capable of doing, and their leadership is strong.

Knowing yourself is a long and involved process, but it is foundational to effective leading. Describe two or three past experiences that helped equip you to lead others.

DAY

7

*The supreme quality of leadership
is unquestionably integrity.*

DWIGHT EISENHOWER

Those who lead successfully lead by example, with strong ethics or morals. Focus on your values, for they are the soul of your leadership, and they drive your behavior. Before you can grow as a leader, you must have a clear understanding of your values and commit to living consistently by them. I believe you should settle what you believe in three key areas: your ethical values, relational values, and success values. If you commit yourself to living your values in these three areas, you'll be well on your way to developing the integrity that makes you attractive to team members and makes them want to follow your leadership.

What does it mean to do the right thing for the right reason (ethical values)? How do you build an environment of trust and respect with others (relational values)? What goals are worth spending your life on (success values)?

DAY

8

It's not what you do once in a while;
it's what you do day in and day out
that makes a difference.

JENNY CRAIG

If you want to become a better leader, you must not only know yourself and define your values. You must also live your values out through the kinds of good habits and systems you consistently practice. Your values should be reflected in your self-leadership, your work ethic, and the kind of example you set. Your values should set the standard for how you treat people through your words and actions. It's up to you to define it. And the earlier you are on the leadership journey, the greater the potential for gain if you start developing good habits now.

Write a
declaration of
commitment
to live out your
values and
what you will
do to grow
as a leader.
Then sign and
date it.

....
....
....
....
....
....
....
....

....
....
....
....
....
....
....
....
....
....
....
....
....
....

DAY

9

*Become the kind of leader that people would follow
voluntarily; even if you had no title or position.*

BRIAN TRACY

In my first leadership position, I mistakenly thought that being named the leader meant that I was the leader. Back then I defined *leading* as a noun—as the position I was appointed to—not a verb—as what I was doing. Though I had been hired as the senior pastor, I quickly discovered the real leader of the church was a down-to-earth farmer named Claude, who had been earning his leadership influence through many positive actions over many years. He later explained it to me, saying, "John, all the letters before or after a name are like the tail on a pig. It has nothing to do with the quality of the bacon." In other words, leadership is action, not position. Leaders are always taking people somewhere. They aren't static. If there is no journey, there is no leadership.

In what ways do you find yourself defining your leadership by position rather than action? How can you change?

DAY

10

*The key to successful leadership today is influence,
not authority.*

KENNETH BLANCHARD

Leadership is influence, and leadership—of any kind, in any location, for any purpose—requires that you take the time and effort to work well *with* people. You must take into account the fact that all people have hopes, dreams, desires, and goals of their own. If you are their leader, you must bring together your vision and the aspirations of your people in a way that benefits everyone. It requires you to know your people, believe in your people, and support your people. You value them as assets rather than liabilities.

Leadership is about working with people. List three actions you could take to improve on your skill in working well with your people. Try to do at least one of them this week.

DAY

Nearly all men can stand adversity, but if you want to test a man's character, give him power.

ABRAHAM LINCOLN

Any time new leaders receive authority, they can be tempted to use it for personal advantage. Let's face it: power can be exhilarating, if not downright intoxicating. But keep this in mind: Just because you have the right to do something as a leader doesn't mean that it is the right thing to do. Each of us as leaders must strive to grow up and grow into a leadership role without relying on our rights or abusing our authority. When you mature in leadership, you will start to change your focus from enjoying authority for its own sake to using authority to serve others.

Are there areas in your leadership or influence where you need to change your focus from rights to responsibilities? Describe the changes you should make to better serve others.

DAY

12

Management is about arranging and telling.
Leadership is about nurturing and enhancing.

Tom Peters

Have you ever heard, "It's lonely at the top"? Despite what you may have been told, leadership doesn't have to be lonely. People make it that way when they misunderstand the functions and purpose of leadership. Being a good leader doesn't mean trying to be king of the hill, setting yourself apart from others. It's not about an us-versus-them culture, with the leader standing alone on top. Good leadership is about walking beside people and helping them to climb up the hill with you. If you're atop the hill alone, you will get lonely. If you have others alongside you, it's hard to be that way.

In what ways do you see yourself walking beside your people, and in what ways are you standing alone as king of the hill? How must you change?

DAY

13

*One of the tests of leadership is the ability to recognize
a problem before it becomes an emergency.*

ARNOLD GLASOW

As a leader at any level, you must deal with the reality that every organization has turnover. It is inevitable. The question every leader must ask is, "Who is leaving my area?" Are the best people departing? Or the average or below-average people? If the best are leaving and below-average are coming in, you need to stop and evaluate why. Good leaders and workers, who often take a job because they want to be part of a particular company, almost always quit because they want to get away from poor leaders and bad work environments. If good people are leaving, odds are high that they did not leave their job. They left the people they had to work with. People quit people, not companies.

Describe the turnover quality of people within your area. Does that tell you anything about your leadership style?

DAY

14

You can buy a man's time; you can buy his physical presence . . . But you cannot buy enthusiasm . . . you cannot buy loyalty . . . you cannot buy the devotion of hearts, minds, or souls. You must earn these.

CLARENCE FRANCIS

When the people who work with you never want to work a moment beyond quitting time and do just enough to get by—to get paid and to keep their job—something is not working. Physically present but mentally absent individuals are highly damaging to your organization because their attitude seems to spread to others. To achieve any level of success as a leader, you must work hard to earn more than "just enough" from your people. Success demands more than most people are willing to offer, but not more than they are capable of giving. The thing that often makes the difference is good leadership.

What positive actions can you take to encourage and motivate people on the team to give their best? Is there something you can do today? If yes, do it. If not today, figure out when and mark it on your calendar.

DAY

15

You don't lead by pointing and telling people some place to go. You lead by going to that place and making a case.

KEN KESEY

Good leaders rely on their people skills to get things done. They treat the individuals being led as people, not mere subordinates. If you want to become a better leader, a people-oriented leader, the following words must be central in your thinking:

- *Side by side*—"Let's work together."
- *Initiative*—"I'll come to you."
- *Inclusion*—"What do you think?"
- *Cooperation*—"Together we can win."
- *Servanthood*—"I'm here to help you."
- *Development*—"I want to add value to you."
- *Encouragement*—"I believe you can do this!"
- *Innovation*—"Let's think outside the box."

In light of these qualities of a people-oriented leader, write an honest review of your current people skills.

DAY

16

Leadership is the capacity to
translate vision into reality.

WARREN BENNIS

I've learned that good leaders don't take anything for granted. They understand that leadership must be earned and established. They remain dissatisfied in a way, because dissatisfaction is a good one-word definition for motivation. Good leaders strive to keep the people and the organization moving forward toward the vision. They must be willing to give up what is in order to reach for what could be. Let a vision for making a difference in the lives of the people you lead lift you and your people above the confines of job descriptions and petty rules. It's time to start moving—and taking others along with you.

Write down the vision of your organization and how your team or department helps to contribute to that vision. Then write down specific ways you can make it easier for your team members to do their part to fulfill the vision. Add these items to your To Do list.

DAY

17

Let him that would move the world,
first move himself.

Socrates

Good leaders understand that it is their responsibility to move toward their people. Leaders are initiators. If you want to improve your leadership, you need to get out of your territory. You need to come down from your high place or leave your office, and find your people. You must move beyond your job description and comfort zone, both in terms of the work you do and the way you interact with your people. You must make it your responsibility to learn who your people are, find out what they need, and help them and the team win. Leadership involves taking risks in your involvement with people, which can be frightening. But know this: the risks are well worth the rewards.

How well do you know your team members? List them and write what you know about them: family, aspirations, interests, history, and goals. For any people you don't know well, make time to learn more about them. Try to talk to at least one of them this week.

DAY

You don't need a title to be a leader.

MULTIPLE ATTRIBUTIONS

Although our culture values titles, the truth is that titles are ultimately empty, and you must learn to see them that way. People who make it their career goals to gain certain titles or positions are not setting themselves up to be the best leaders they can be. The person you are and the work you do are what really matters. If the work is significant and adds value to people, then it doesn't need to come with a title. Developing an awareness that position is the lowest level of leadership brings a healthy sense of dissatisfaction with the title as well as a desire to grow and create positive change. A position is not a worthy destination for any person's life; it is only the starting point on your leadership journey.

What can you do to identify more with how you contribute to the team or organization?

DAY

Outstanding leaders go out of their way to boost the self-esteem of their personnel. If people believe in themselves, it's amazing what they can accomplish.

SAM WALTON

If you want to become a better leader, you can't focus on rules and procedures to get things done or keep things going. You must develop relationships. Why? Because the reality is that the people get things done, not the playbook they use. And because people are the power behind any organization, they are its most valuable—and appreciable—asset. It takes time to develop your people skills, but it takes no time at all to let others know that you value them, expressing appreciation for them and taking interest in them personally. That's a positive change you can make quickly with immediate benefits!

Think about the people you lead. Pick one, and in front of others on the team, tell him or her the value they bring. Note their response here. Try to get in the habit of doing this with everyone on your team.

DAY

20

Ask your team—they know the answer.

CHUCK CARLSON

Insecurity and immaturity can cause a leader to act like The Answer Man or Woman. However, this is positional thinking. Good leaders think differently. They know a leader's job is not to know everything but to attract people who know things that he or she does not. In my own growth in leadership, once I recognized that one of us is not as smart as all of us, I stopped bringing people together to give them answers and started calling on them to help us find answers. Doing that will transform your leadership, not only because you can be yourself and stop pretending that you know more than you do, but also because it will harness the power of shared thinking.

What questions are you being asked that you cannot answer? Who on your team can help provide answers and make problem solving more collaborative? Schedule a time to meet with these people.

DAY

21

If you want help, help others. If you want trust, trust others. If you want love, give it away. If you want friends, be one. If you want a great team, be a great teammate. That's how it works.

DAN ZADRA

To improve as a leader, you must develop your skills for working with others. Good leadership means relating well to other people. It requires leaders to be examples for other people. It challenges them to develop and equip people. Good leadership is about collaboration, inclusion, and sacrifice of selfish personal ambition for the sake of the team and the vision of the organization. It means being part of something greater than yourself. It means putting others ahead of yourself and being willing to move slowly enough to take the people you lead with you. Once you decide to include others in the leadership journey, you are well on your way to achieving success.

Do you ever sacrifice positive interaction with people in order to get your work done? If so, you are undermining your leadership. How can you change to put more value on others and your interaction with them?

DAY

Leadership is an opportunity to serve.

J. DONALD WALTERS

Leaders often focus their efforts on serving themselves or their organization, with too little regard for others. Leaders who improve shift their focus from *me* to *we*. They like people and treat them as individuals. They develop relationships and win people over with interaction instead of using the power of their position. That shift in attitude creates a positive change in the working environment. The workplace becomes friendlier. People begin to like one another. Chemistry starts to develop on the team. People no longer possess a "have to" mindset. Instead it turns to "want to." The workplace becomes more enjoyable for everyone—leaders and followers alike.

What adjectives would you use to describe how the people you work with generally behave and interact? Circle the adjectives that apply to you as well. Are they positive words? Which ones do you need to change?

DAY

*The best minute you spend is the
one you invest in people.*

KENNETH BLANCHARD
AND SPENCER JOHNSON

Spending time with the people I love—whether at work, at home, or while playing—is my greatest joy, and it always energizes me. You see, good relationships create energy and give an environment a positive feel. When you invest time and effort to get to know people and build good relationships, it actually pays off with greater energy once the relationships are built. When people feel liked, cared for, included, valued, and trusted, they begin to work together with their leader and one another. And in that kind of positive, energetic environment, people are willing to give their best because they know the leader wants the best for them.

How can you more effectively invest yourself in the lives of those you lead? What step will you take today to ensure that people feel cared for and valued?

DAY

24

*Above all else, good leaders are open. They go up,
down, and around their organizations to reach people.
They don't stick to established channels. They're informal.
They're straight with people. They make a religion
out of being accessible.*

JACK WELCH

Are you a good listener to your people? Recently I came across an explanation of the Chinese symbol for the verb "to listen," which is made up of smaller symbols that stand for *you*, *eyes*, *heart*, *ear*, and *undivided attention*. When I open up the channels of communication and really listen, here is what I must give others:

- *Ears*—I hear what you say.
- *Eyes*—I see what you say.
- *Heart*—I feel what you say.
- *Undivided attention*—I value who you are and what you say.

Only when we do these things are we able to build positive relationships and persuade people to follow us.

How are your listening skills? What can you do to create an environment where people begin to communicate with you and one another openly?

DAY

25

When there is danger, a good leader takes the front line. But when there is celebration, a good leader stays in the back room. If you want the cooperation of human beings around you, make them feel that they are important.

NELSON MANDELA

Good leadership is relationally driven. That is only possible when people respect and value one another as important. It is impossible to relate well with those you don't respect. When respect lessens in a relationship, the relationship diminishes. You can care for people without leading them, but you cannot lead them effectively without caring for them. As a leader, you can lift the value bar in your area. You just have to make the decision to do it. You need to let the people know that they matter, that you see them as individual human beings, not just workers. This attitude makes a positive impact on people, and it strengthens your leadership.

Is there anyone with whom you have difficulty working? Think about why that is. What can you do to improve that relationship?

DAY

26

When the crunch comes, people cling to those they know they can trust—those who are not detached, but involved.

JAMES STOCKDALE

The path to leadership growth requires that one stops trying to impress others to maintain their position and starts developing trust to maintain their relationships. If you have integrity with people, you develop trust. The more trust you develop, the stronger the relationship becomes. The better the relationship, the greater the potential for a leader to gain permission to lead. It's a building process that takes time, energy, and intentionality. In times of difficulty, relationships are a shelter. In times of opportunity, they are a launching pad. Trust is required for people to feel safe enough to create, share, question, attempt, and risk. Without it, leadership is weak and teamwork is impossible.

How much trust have you developed with your team? Do your people feel safe to create, share, question, attempt, and risk? What can you do to earn greater trust?

DAY

27

I cannot give you the formula for success,
but I can give you the formula for failure, which is:
Try to please everybody.

HERBERT SWOPE

When I started my leadership career, I quickly built relationships with people, but I fell into the trap of wanting to make only decisions that were approved and accepted by all. It took a crisis in my leadership for me to realize that I was a people pleaser. My goal had been to make everyone happy. That was the wrong goal. As a leader, my goal should have been to help people, not to make them happy. That realization changed my leadership. For the first time I was freed up. I was no longer held captive by every person's opinion, which was a very unhealthy place to be. I could focus on doing what I believed was best for the organization and the people. Making everyone happy isn't responsible. Nor is it even possible. If you're like me, you may need to add the "hard" side of leadership that makes difficult decisions.

Think of an instance when you sacrificed what you thought was best for the popular choice. How could you have handled the situation differently? Is there a decision you are currently facing in which you can apply what you learned?

DAY

28

*In real life, the most practical advice for leaders is
not to treat pawns like pawns, nor princes like princes,
but all persons like persons.*

JAMES MACGREGOR BURNS

In a hard-charging, high-performance, leadership-intensive environment, leading by being relational and caring for people can be seen as weak, especially if you possess a natural bias toward action (rather than affection). For that reason, some people dismiss it. What a mistake—and what a handicap to their leadership potential. If you started your leadership focused on the "hard" aspects of leadership, meaning the productivity side, without being relational, you may make a small degree of progress in the beginning, but you'll fall short in the long run because you'll either alienate your people or burn them out. You can't become successful in leadership until you learn both.

Are you an achiever who tends to put productivity ahead of people? How can you move toward becoming more relational?

DAY

29

The fields of industry are strewn with the bones of those organizations whose leadership became infested with dry rot, who believed in taking instead of giving ... who didn't realize that the only assets that could not be replaced easily were the human ones.

LE ROY H. KURTZ

High achievers want to get things done and get them done *now*! They usually don't want to slow down for anything or anyone. But the valuable process of building relationships takes time. It can be very slow work. If you're a high achiever, you may be saying to yourself, *I haven't needed to develop relationships to be a good leader.* Here is my answer to that: as long as you're winning, people are willing to follow—even if you are hard on them. However, when you drive people to achieve without slowing down to build relationships, a part of them will want to see you lose. Keep in mind the saying that if you step on people's fingers on the way up, they may trip you on the way down.

In what ways and with which team members do you need to slow down and build relationships? What will you do to improve those relationships?

DAY

30

Trust men and they will be true to you; treat them greatly,
and they will show themselves great.

RALPH WALDO EMERSON

When leaders are relational, their followers naturally get close to them. That sometimes means that they mistake kindness for weakness. They believe that encouragement means they don't have to respect boundaries. They assume that empowerment means they have the freedom to do whatever they want. As a result, they take advantage of their leaders. Being relational is a risk that can result in some lifelong disappointments but also lifelong friendships that you will cherish deeply. It gives you the chance to have deep, rewarding relationships that will enrich your life and the lives of others. I hope you will choose to build relationships. I made that choice early in my leadership life, and though I have been hurt and I've occasionally had others take advantage of me, I don't regret it. Most people respect the relationship, treat it the right way, and add great value to me.

Have you ever felt someone took advantage of you because of your relationship with that person? How did you handle the situation? What might you do differently if faced with a similar situation today?

DAY

31

*The most essential quality for leadership is not perfection
but credibility. People must be able to trust you.*

RICK WARREN

Most people don't want to admit their mistakes,
expose their faults, and face up to their shortcomings.
They don't get too close to people lest they be discovered. And if people enter into leadership, the urge to
hide their weaknesses can become even stronger. Most
people believe they must show greater strength as leaders. However, if leaders try to maintain a façade with the
people they lead, they cannot build authentic relationships. Author and pastor Rick Warren observes, "You can
impress people from a distance, but you must get close
to influence them." To develop authentic relationships of
influence, leaders need to be authentic. They must admit
their mistakes and faults and shortcomings. In other
words, they must be the real deal. That is a vulnerable
place to be for a leader.

Have you been afraid to be vulnerable with your team? What do you feel are your vulnerabilities? How can you build more authenticity with your team members?

DAY

32

*Leadership is practiced not so much in words
as in attitude and in actions.*

HAROLD S. GENEEN

Perhaps you are not naturally gifted at working with people. In fact, you may struggle with liking some people enough to commit the energy needed to make good connections with them. If you have difficulty with this, do the following: *Make a choice to care about others.* Liking people and caring about people is a choice within your control. If you haven't already, make that choice. Look for something that is likable about every person you meet. It's there. Make it your job to find it and then to express what you like about that person, especially your team members.

Make a list of all your team members and write down the qualities you admire in each of them. How do those qualities make each of them valuable to the team?

DAY

33

*Why is it that I always get the whole person when
what I really want is a pair of hands?*
HENRY FORD

Let's face it: relationships are messy. Many leaders would rather deal with people only in terms of their work life. But the reality is that when you lead someone, you always get the whole person—including their dysfunctions, home life, health issues, and quirks. The messiness of people problems can lead to disillusionment and discouragement and make leadership troublesome. However, good leaders understand that the heart of leadership is dealing with people and working with the good, the bad, and the ugly in everyone. They are able to look at hard truths, see people's flaws, face reality, and do it in a spirit of grace and truth. They don't avoid problems; they solve them. Leaders who build relationships understand that conflict is a part of progress. Often it is even constructive.

Are there problems with team members that you are avoiding rather than solving? Name one problem that you will deal with today and how you will approach it.

DAY

34

Looking back, my life seems like one big obstacle race,
with me being the chief obstacle.

JACK PAAR

One of the secrets of connecting with people and building relationships is knowing and liking yourself. In my book *Winning with People*, I call it the Mirror Principle, which says, "The first person we must examine is ourselves." The work in relationship building always has to start with yourself. That means you must become a student of yourself. Learn your strengths and weaknesses. Understand the way you think, feel, and act in every kind of situation. It also means that you be honest with yourself and take responsibility to do the things that will change your life for the better. Then once you know who you are, forget about yourself and place your focus on others. You will relate to other people from a place of strength.

Write an honest review of your strengths and weaknesses. What areas of your life can you change for the better? What actions will you take and when?

DAY

35

*Leadership and learning are
indispensable to each other.*

JOHN FITZGERALD KENNEDY

Those who lead people effectively don't rely on rules or depend on systems. They work with people's emotions. They think more in terms of human capacity and less in terms of regulations. They think more in terms of buy-in and less in terms of procedures. And they never try to rule with a stick. (Anyone who does needs to know that every stick eventually breaks.) Instead, they use a personal touch whenever they deal with people. They listen, learn, and then lead. They develop relationships. They have more than an open-door policy—they know the door swings both ways. They go through it and get out among their people to connect.

What would you say a "personal touch" from you looks like to your people? List three actions you can take to connect with your people today.

DAY

36

*Leading an organization is as much about soul
as it is about systems. Effective leadership finds
its source in understanding.*

HERB KELLEHER

To achieve progress, good leaders never take the human factor out of the equation in anything they do. They always take people into account—where they are, what they believe, what they're feeling. Every question they ask is expressed in the context of people. Knowing what to do isn't enough to make someone a good leader. Just because something is right doesn't necessarily mean that people will let you do it. Good leaders take that into account, then they think and plan accordingly. And to accomplish this, you must exhibit a consistent mood, maintain an optimistic attitude, possess a listening ear, and present to others your authentic self.

Describe what each of your team members value and want or hope for in their lives. Don't know? Finding out—it's vital to building relationships.

DAY

37

Whatever you want men to do to you, do also to them.

JESUS CHRIST

While you always want to be motivating people, there is a fine line between manipulating people for personal gain and motivating them for mutual benefit. Good leaders can keep that tendency in check and keep from crossing over from motivation to manipulation by following the golden rule: "Treat others as you want others to treat you." That simple rule can be universally understood and followed and is the simplest, most profound, and most positive guide to living there is. Practicing the golden rule in leadership enables everyone to feel respected. That changes the entire environment of a department or an organization. When leaders change from driving people to respecting people, their people go from feeling like a stake to feeling like a stakeholder.

List three actions you will do today to treat others the way you would like them to treat you.

DAY

*Kind words can be short and easy to speak,
but their echoes are endless.*

MOTHER TERESA

One day Truett Cathy, the founder of Chick-fil-A, said to me, "Do you know how I identify someone who needs encouragement? If the person is breathing, they need a pat on the back!" I have yet to meet a person who doesn't enjoy and benefit from encouragement. As a leader, you have great power to lift people up through encouragement. The words "I'm glad you work with me; you add incredible value to the team" mean a lot coming from someone who has the best interests of the team, department, or organization at heart. If you want people to be positive and to always be glad when they see you coming, encourage them. If you become the chief encourager of the people on your team, they will work hard and strive to meet your positive expectations.

Write down one positive thing you can honestly say about each person on your team. Then take the time during this next week to compliment each person with it.

DAY

39

Effective leadership is not about making speeches or being liked; leadership is defined by results not attributes.

PETER DRUCKER

Some people think that in order to build solid relationships, they need to treat the people on their team like family. Others think being a caring leader means giving team members permission to do whatever they want. Both are wrong. People don't deal realistically with their family. I don't. I have a commitment level with them that is deeper than with others. Regardless of what they do, I am committed to giving them unconditional love. They have privileges that I extend to no other people. And compromise is a constant. What makes a family great isn't what makes a team great. Families value community over contribution. Businesses value contribution over community. The best teams strike a balance.

Do you have a team member who constantly wants to be treated as a "family member"? What can you say to repair the balance between this person's contribution and sense of community?

DAY

40

*A good objective of leadership is to help those who
are doing poorly to do well and to help those who
are doing well to do even better.*

JIM ROHN

Every person has problems and makes mistakes in the workplace. Every person needs to improve and needs someone to come alongside them to help them improve. As a leader, it is your responsibility and your privilege to be the person who helps them get better. I believe that people can change their attitudes and can improve their abilities. And because I do, I talk to them about where they're coming up short. If you're a leader and you want to help people, you need to be willing to have those tough, candid conversations. So how does a leader handle being relational while still trying to move people forward? By balancing care and candor. Care without candor creates dysfunctional relationships. Candor without care creates distant relationships. But care balanced with candor creates developing relationships.

When a person in your area has problems, do you tend to show care without candor or candor without care? What can you do to change that to care balanced with candor?

DAY

41

Faithful are the wounds of a friend,
but deceitful are the kisses of an enemy.

To lead successfully, it is important for you to value people. That is foundational to solid relationships. Caring for others demonstrates that you value them. However, if you want to help them get better, you have to be honest about where they need to improve. That shows that you value the person's potential. That requires candor. One of the secrets of being candid is to think, speak, and act in terms of who the person has the potential to become and to think about how you can help them to reach it. Being candid doesn't have to be harmful. It can be similar to the work of a surgeon. It may hurt, but it is meant to help and it shouldn't harm. As a leader, you must be willing and able to do that. If not, you won't be able to help your people grow and change.

Consider a candid conversation you have had that did not lead to a positive result. If you could redo the conversation, what might you say differently to emphasize the person's potential and how you could help them reach it?

DAY

42

To command is to serve,
nothing more and nothing less.

ANDRE MALRAUX

To help you keep the balance between care and candor, I've created a caring candor checklist for working with people. If you can answer yes to the following questions before having a candid conversation, then your motives are probably right and you have a good chance of being able to communicate effectively.

- ○ Have I invested enough in the relationship to be candid with them?
- ○ Do I truly value them as people?
- ○ Am I sure this is their issue and not mine?
- ○ Am I sure I'm not speaking up because I feel threatened?
- ○ Is the issue more important than the relationship?
- ○ Does this conversation clearly serve their interests and not just mine?
- ○ Am I willing to invest time and energy to help them change?
- ○ Am I willing to show them how to do something, not just say what's wrong?
- ○ Am I willing and able to set clear, specific expectations?

Consider a team member whom you need to have a candid conversation with, then go through the caring candor checklist and write out your answers.

DAY

43

A most important key to successful leadership is your ability to direct and challenge the very best that is in those whom you lead.

UNKNOWN

Most leaders I talk to have a difficult conversation that they know they need to have but are avoiding. Usually they are reluctant for one of two reasons: either they don't like confrontation, or they fear that they will hurt the person they need to talk to. The reality is that not everyone responds well to candid conversations. Let's face it: honesty can hurt. The next time you find yourself in a place where you need to have a candid conversation, just remember this:

- *Do it quickly*—shovel the pile while it's small.
- *Do it calmly, never in anger*—use the caring candor checklist.
- *Do it privately*—you want to help the person, not embarrass him or her.
- *Do it thoughtfully*, in a way that minimizes embarrassment or intimidation.

Are you avoiding a difficult conversation you know a team member needs? Why? What step will you take today to discuss it with them?

DAY

44

*Good leadership involves responsibility to the
welfare of the group, which means that some people
will get angry at your actions and decisions.
It's inevitable—if you're honorable.*

COLIN POWELL

Solid relationships are defined by how people care
about one another. But just because people care about
one another doesn't mean that they are going anywhere
together. Getting the team moving together to accomplish a goal is the responsibility of the leader, and that
often requires candor. My friend, Colin Sewell, owner
of several auto dealerships, said to me, "Leaders have to
make the best decisions for the largest group of people.
Therefore, leaders give up the right to cater to an individual if it hurts the team or the organization." Getting
results always matters, and good leaders never lose track
of that. If you want to lead people well, you need to be
willing to direct them candidly.

Do you find yourself catering to an individual or individuals to the detriment of your team? What action do you need to take to change this?

DAY

45

*A true leader has to have a genuine open-door
policy so that his people are not afraid to
approach him for any reason.*

HAROLD S. GENEEN

As you work with people and have candid conversations, allow me to remind you of one more thing: can-
didness is a two-way street. If you want to be an effective
leader and earn your people's trust, you must allow the
people you work with to be candid with you. You must
solicit feedback. And you must be mature and secure
enough to take in people's criticism without defensive-
ness and learn from it. Leadership expert Warren Bennis
observed, "Effective leaders reward dissent, as well as
encourage it. They understand that whatever momentary
discomfort they experience as a result of being told from
time to time that they are wrong is more than offset by
the fact that 'reflective back talk' increases a leader's ability to make good decisions." Caring for people, making
good decisions for everyone involved, and building solid
relationships are what good leadership is all about.

What do you do to ensure that your people are not afraid to approach you for any reason? Who among your team members can you solicit feedback from?

DAY

46

You can dream, create, design, and build the most wonderful idea in the world, but it requires people to make the dream a reality.

WALT DISNEY

Leaders are by nature visionary. They have great hopes and big dreams. They want to win, and win big. But a great vision without a great team often turns into a nightmare. Teamwork makes the dream work. Often leaders share their visions with me and then ask, "Do you think my people will buy into my vision?" When they ask me this, I know the question they should be asking is, "Have my people bought into me?" The size or the worthiness of a leader's vision often isn't what determines whether it will be achieved. Before you ask people to move forward to achieve the vision, they must first buy into you as the leader. Before they buy into you as the leader, you must have earned their trust and gained permission to lead them.

Have you gained your people's permission to lead them? What do you base your answer upon? How can you improve on earning their trust?

DAY

47

A leader takes people where they want to go.
A great leader takes people where they don't
necessarily want to go, but ought to be.

Rosalynn Carter

To succeed as a leader, you have to be willing to risk what you've developed relationally for the sake of the bigger picture. If achieving the vision is worth building the team, it is also worth risking the relationships, but this creates tension for a leader. That tension will force you to make a choice: to shrink the vision or to stretch the people trying to achieve it. If you want to do big things, you need to take people out of their comfort zones. They might fail. They might relieve their own tension by fighting you or quitting. If you risk and win, then your people gain confidence, trust increases, and the team is ready to take on even more difficult challenges. However, if you risk and fail, you lose relational credibility with your people and you will have to rebuild the relationships. But there is no progress without risk, so you need to get used to it.

In what ways are you stretching your people to achieve the vision for your area? What more can you risk to take them out of their comfort zones?

DAY

48

The outstanding leaders of every age are those who set up their own quotas and constantly exceed them.

THOMAS WATSON

Production qualifies and separates true leaders from people who merely occupy leadership positions. Good leaders always make things happen. They get results. They can make a significant impact on an organization. Not only are they productive individually, but they create momentum and develop an environment of success, which makes the team better and stronger and more productive. No one can fake this. Either you're producing for the organization and adding to its bottom line (whatever that may be), or you're not. If you desire to grow as a leader, you simply have to produce. There is no other way around it.

*How are results
measured
in your
organization?
Find a way
to measure
your personal
contribution,
and the
contribution
of your team.*

DAY

49

There are two types of people in the business community: those who produce results and those who give you reasons why they didn't.

PETER DRUCKER

The ability to produce results has always been the separation line for success. It is also the qualifying line for leadership. Authentic leaders know the way and show the way to productivity. Their leadership talk is supported by their walk. They deliver results. They live on their performance, not their potential. They lead by example. And their ability to get results tends to silence their critics and build their reputations. Good leaders *take* their people where they want them to go—they don't *send* them there. They are more like tour guides than travel agents. Why? Because people always believe what we do more than what we say. Therefore the credibility of a leader can be summed up in one word: *example.*

List the qualities you consider your strengths. Where do you shine the most? How can you further develop those qualities?

DAY

*Example is not the main thing in influencing others,
it is the only thing.*

ALBERT SCHWEITZER

Producers and achievers always have an impact on the people who work with them and for them. Productivity puts people at the head of the class. And when that producer has already done the slower work of building relationships, his or her leadership really takes off! This is true because productive leaders are an example to the people they lead, and their productivity sets the standard for the team. President Abraham Lincoln recognized this. During the American Civil War, the president relieved General John C. Fremont of his command for this reason: "His cardinal mistake is that he isolates himself and allows no one to see him." Lincoln knew that leaders need to be among their people, inspiring them with their ability, letting them see what the standard should be for their performance. When leaders produce, so do their people. Productive leaders thrive on results—from themselves and the team. They show the way and others follow.

How do you communicate the status of your goals and your achievements to your team? In what ways can you more intentionally show your performance and set an example for others to follow?

DAY

51

Leadership is the capacity to translate vision into reality.

WARREN BENNIS

Good leaders constantly communicate the vision of the organization. They do it clearly, creatively, and continually. But that doesn't mean that everyone who receives the message understands and embraces it. The effective leader also communicates the vision through action, which helps people understand it in ways they may not have before. When followers see positive results and see goals being met, they get a clearer picture of what it means to fulfill the vision. And with each day of productivity, the team gets one step closer to making the vision a reality. That encourages members of the team. It validates their efforts. It makes the vision that much clearer. And clarity is compelling. Productivity also expands the vision, because with increased confidence and skill, the people doing the work recognize that they can actually accomplish more than they may have believed was possible.

When was the last time you cast vision to your team? Carefully consider and write down the vision and define its success, then communicate it creatively as often and in as many ways as possible.

DAY

52

Morale is the state of mind. It is steadfastness and
courage and hope. It is confidence and zeal and loyalty. . . .
It is staying power, the spirit that endures to the end—
the will to win. With it all things are possible,
without it everything else . . . is for naught.

GEORGE C. MARSHALL

Many people in leadership positions try to solve problems by using systems. Or they pay others to try to solve problems for them. But the truth is, leaders cannot delegate the solving of problems to someone else. They have to be active in breaking through obstacles, putting out fires, correcting mistakes, and directing people. Good leaders do that. Historian and essayist Thomas Carlyle observed, "Nothing builds self-esteem and self-confidence like accomplishment." And once their effectiveness becomes contagious and spreads throughout the team, productivity begins to solve many problems—many more than management or consultants ever will. Productivity is inspiring. People who feel good about themselves often produce good results. And good results create positive momentum and high morale for a long time.

In what ways are you coming alongside your people and helping to solve problems? What more can you do to help them improve their productivity and raise morale?

DAY

53

When you win, nothing hurts.

JOE NAMATH

What's the most effective way to solve problems? Using momentum. How does a leader create momentum? By helping the team get wins under its belt. If you're not thinking in terms of helping your team win, then you aren't thinking like a leader. Find small challenges for individual team members to take on in order to experience individual wins. Then look for obtainable challenges for people to win together as a team. The greater the number of wins there are both individually and corporately, the more you can increase the difficulty of the challenges. And the more momentum you can gain.

Think of a small challenge for each member of your team to help them build confidence and spark momentum. Is there a way to translate those wins into a larger goal for the team?

DAY

54

*If you're coasting, you're either losing momentum
or else you're headed downhill.*

JOAN WELSH

When well-led organizations sustain high morale and high productivity over time, they gain momentum, which is any leader's best friend. Momentum helps a leader do anything and everything more easily. That's why I call it the great exaggerator. Without momentum, everything is harder to do than it should be. With it, everything is easier. The same can be said of leadership momentum. Have it on your side, and your performance is actually better than your capability. For example, think about what happened with Apple when the company introduced the iPhone. It created a tidal wave of momentum and vastly increased their market share, not only in smartphones but also in computers. After years of being marginalized as a niche company with a relatively small but very loyal following, they are now mainstream again and going strong. That's why I often advise leaders to spend more time trying to create momentum.

How would you rate the current level of morale and productivity in your area? What can you and your team do to raise those levels and start building momentum?

DAY

Don't worry about making friends; don't worry about making enemies. Worry about winning, because if you win, your enemies can't hurt you, and if you lose, your friends can't stand you.

PAUL "BEAR" BRYANT

Effective leaders understand momentum and use it to the organization's advantage. And they also understand that there are three types of people when it comes to momentum. *Momentum takers* don't start or stop anything, and their productivity and effectiveness are based almost entirely on what others do to make things happen in the organization. For that reason, they need good leaders who produce and create a productive environment. *Momentum breakers* hurt morale, cause problems, and not only do they not produce, but they prevent others from producing. *Momentum makers* are leaders who produce and make things happen, creating momentum. You need to put the majority of your time and energy into the momentum makers and place them strategically in your area so that they make the greatest impact.

Who among your team members do you regard as momentum makers? How can you invest more time and energy into their development and gain the greatest impact?

DAY

56

*The way a team plays as a whole determines its
success. You may have the greatest bunch of individual
stars in the world, but if they don't play together,
the club won't be worth a dime.*

BABE RUTH

Leadership credibility grows when you and your team are productive. In most organizations, that makes you winners, and winners attract people—some good, some bad, some average. The key to building a winning team is recognizing, selecting, and retaining the best people from the ones you attract. However, having talented people on the team doesn't automatically guarantee success. You can still lose with good players, but you cannot win without them. The difference comes from building them into a team. That will take time. But remember this: if you aren't a proven producer, you won't attract and keep other proven producers. That's why you need to produce personally and lead by example.

Who are the producers on your team? Do they work well with others or are they more independent? For those who tend toward independence, what can you do to encourage them toward a more team-oriented mentality?

DAY

57

*The basic building block of good team-building is
for a leader to promote the feeling that every
human being is unique and adds value.*

Unknown

All great leaders are productive. However, it is possible to be a producer and not a leader. Personal success does not always translate into team success. Leadership is defined by what a person does with and for others. It is established by making the team better and more productive. It's measured by what the entire group accomplishes, not by the individual efforts of the person in charge. Good leadership is never based on what someone does by and for himself. I've seen someone make things happen, and I thought, *Wow, this person is going to be a fantastic leader*, only to have that person continue to make things happen for himself but ignore and demoralize his team. That's not leadership. A prerequisite for being an effective leader is the ability to be effective yourself, but good leaders must go beyond being productive and possess the desire to take the entire team to a higher level.

Define what success means to you as a leader. Write an honest review of how you are currently taking your team to a higher level.

DAY

58

*No leader, however great, can long
continue unless he wins victories.*

BERNARD LAW MONTGOMERY

I once saw a cartoon depicting a sales meeting in which the speaker said, "We run our business like a game show—produce and you come back, don't produce and we have some lovely parting gifts for you." That's humorous, but that's also the way it is for leaders. Productivity is measurable. Organizational growth is tangible. Profitability is quantifiable. Leaders who fail to increase them are held accountable. Leaders who add to them are rewarded—and then asked to achieve even more the next time. High performance requires high commitment. Effective leaders understand that the cost of leadership is carrying the responsibility of their team's success on their shoulders. As you improve your productivity, that is an increased weight you must embrace and carry.

You need inner strength to persevere and carry out your responsibilities. What sources bring you renewal and inspiration? How can you make them a priority in your life?

DAY

59

Be willing to make decisions.
That's the most important quality in a good leader.

T. BOONE PICKENS

Whenever you see a thriving organization, you can be sure that its leaders made some very tough decisions—and are continuing to make them. Success is an uphill journey. People don't coast their way to effective leadership. If you want to lead at a higher level, be ready to make difficult decisions. As strong relationships are being built, you will have to start making difficult people decisions. As productivity takes off, you'll continue to make those but also add difficult production decisions. That makes leadership even more difficult. I've already told you about how difficult I found it to make decisions early in my career. Today as I look back, I regret the decisions I failed to make more than I do the wrong decisions I did make. Don't fall into the same trap I did of postponing decisions when I should have made them.

What difficult decision are you facing today? Have you been postponing the decision? If so, what will you do to move forward on it?

DAY

60

To do right is wonderful. To teach others to do right is even more wonderful—and much easier.

MARK TWAIN

As I established strong relationships and the productivity of my leadership increased, I found most of the difficult decisions I had to make were personal ones that require change, honesty, and self-discipline. As a growing leader, you must make the difficult decision to:

○ Be successful before you try to help others be successful.
○ Hold yourself to a higher standard than you ask of others.
○ Make yourself accountable to others.
○ Set tangible goals and then reach them.
○ Accept responsibility for personal results.
○ Admit failure and mistakes quickly and humbly.
○ Ask from others only what you have previously asked of yourself.
○ Gauge your success on results, not intentions.
○ Remove yourself from situations where you are ineffective.

Going first in these areas of your life may not always be easy or fun, but it is always a leadership requirement that paves the way for the people who follow and increases their chances of success for completing the journey.

Review the list, and put a check mark by those statements that you believe apply to you. What can you do to improve in the areas that remain unchecked?

DAY

61

Do what you do so well that those who see you do what you do are going to come back to see you do it again and tell others that they should see you do what you do.

WALT DISNEY

One of the keys to leadership is understanding how your gifts and abilities can be used productively to further the vision of the organization. Part of that is personal. In previous readings I discussed the importance of knowing yourself and deciding on your personal leadership style. This is slightly different. If you are a leader, you must have a sense of vision for your leadership. And it must align, at least during the current season, with the vision of the organization you serve. Developing a sense of where your true strengths lie and how you can serve in your leadership will take effort, and the process may often be messy. But as you come to understand your special gifts and abilities, you will know what your personal contribution can be to the organization. The more focused you are within your talents, the more rapid the rate of growth and the greater you increase your overall potential to be a productive leader.

What have you come to understand are your special gifts and abilities? How can you become more focused within your talents to better serve your current organization?

*D*AY

62

The very essence of leadership is that you have
to have a vision. It's got to be a vision you articulate
clearly and forcefully on every occasion.
You can't blow an uncertain trumpet.

THEODORE HESBURGH

Vision casting is an integral part of leading. Fuzzy communication leads to unclear direction, which produces sloppy execution. Productive leaders create a clear link between the vision of the organization and everyday production of the team. They define and redefine what success means for the people working there. They show how the short term impacts the long term. They are clear in their communication and continually point the way for their team. A compelling vision is clear and well-defined, expansive and challenging. It is aligned with the shared values of the team. It is focused primarily on the end, not means. It fits the giftedness of the team. And when it is communicated and understood, it fills the room with energy!

When you cast vision to your team, does it fill the room with energy? If not, why not? Take the time to carefully define and redefine the vision and what success means, then deliver it again.

DAY

63

Give all the credit away.

JOHN WOODEN

Few things inspire people like victory. The job of a leader is to help the team succeed. As individuals on the team get to experience small successes, it motivates them to keep going and reach for larger successes. If you want your people to be inspired to win, then reward and celebrate the small daily victories that they achieve. And make them part of your personal victory celebrations whenever possible, giving them as much of the credit as you can. Not only does that motivate people, but it also helps them to enjoy the journey.

List three actions you could take today to highlight and celebrate the small daily successes by individuals in your area.

DAY

64

The job of a leader is to build a complementary team,
where every strength is made effective and
each weakness is made irrelevant.

STEPHEN COVEY

When you have built strong relationships with people in your area, they begin to like *being* together. But when you get the production moving, they begin to *work* together. Production makes team-building possible. That can be accomplished only by a leader who is willing to push forward and lead the way for the people. The ideal that every leader should shoot for is people working together, each bringing their strengths to make the team better and compensating for one another's weaknesses. How does that happen? First, you must know the strengths and weaknesses of each player. Team members should complement one another, and as the leader it is your job to help them figure out how to be successful and to lead them through the process.

Define each team member's area of contribution (including your own). What strengths make each person particularly suited to their current work?

DAY

65

Certainly a leader needs a clear vision of the organization and where it is going, but a vision is of little value unless it is shared in a way so as to generate enthusiasm and commitment. Leadership and communication are inseparable.

CLAUDE TAYLOR

Good leaders never assume that their team members understand the mission. They don't take anything for granted. No doubt that was the reason the legendary NFL coach Vince Lombardi's first speech every season began with the sentence, "This is a football." It's the reason John Wooden, the great UCLA basketball coach, taught his players at the beginning of every season the proper way to put on socks so that they wouldn't sustain foot injuries. They made sure their players knew what they needed to in order to accomplish their mission. Don't take for granted that your team members know what you know or believe what you believe. Don't assume they understand how their talents and efforts are supposed to contribute to the mission of the team. Communicate it often.

Take some time to consider what your team members really need to know to accomplish their missions. Communicate it to them today.

DAY

66

T.E.A.M = Together everyone achieves more.

UNKNOWN

Your team members should receive feedback about their performance, and you need to take responsibility for walking team members through that process. A friend of mine who runs a business decided to call her company together for a mid-year evaluation. On a whiteboard, she wrote three columns: *Did Right—Did Wrong—Will Change.* Being an effective leader, the first thing she did was ask all the people on her team to share their observations, adding her own items to their list only when no one else mentioned them. From this meeting she discovered what her team thought about the work they did and learned things she didn't know that allowed her and the team to be on the same page, and the team took ownership of the rest of the year because their ideas had come from the heart. The process was so effective that it became a regular event every year.

Do you regularly meet with your team to discuss what is going right, what is going wrong, and what needs to change? What can you do to increase your team's willingness to take ownership of their performance?

DAY

67

True leadership lies in guiding others to success.
In ensuring that everyone is performing at their best,
doing the work they are pledged to do and doing it well.

BILL OWENS

Team members should work in an environment conducive to growth and inspiration, and team leaders should create an environment for their people that inspires, challenges, and stretches them. As you lead, you need to make it your goal to lift up others and help them do their best. It is a key to productivity. You set the tone more than anyone else on a team, in a department, or for an organization. Your attitude is contagious. If you are positive, encouraging, and open to growth, so are your people. If you want to succeed, acknowledge the influence you have and use it to everyone's best advantage.

What tone do you set for your team members? Give yourself an honest review. What can you do today to be more positive and encouraging?

DAY

68

... trying to build momentum by doing, doing, doing—and doing more ... rarely works. Those who build the good-to-great companies, however, made as much use of "stop doing" lists as "to do" lists. They displayed a remarkable discipline to unplug all sorts of extraneous junk.

JIM COLLINS

To be an effective leader, you must learn to not only get a lot done, but to get a lot of the right things done. That means understanding how to prioritize time, tasks, resources, and even people. Staying in your areas of strength—where your efforts yield the highest return—and out of your areas of weakness is one of the keys to personal productivity. For years I have relied on the 80/20 rule as a guideline to help me decide what is worth focusing on and what isn't. Every day I list the tasks I must do, then I focus 80 percent of my time on the top 20 percent. To help me understand what my top 20 percent is, I ask myself three questions: What is required of me? (what I must do). What gives me the greatest return? (what I should do). What is most rewarding to me? (what I love to do). Your goal as you grow as a leader is to shift your time and attention to the should-dos and love-to-dos.

How do you prioritize your time and tasks on a daily basis? Utilizing the 80/20 rule, what will your focus look like today?

DAY

69

There is something that is much more scarce, something rarer than ability. It is the ability to recognize ability.

ROBERT HALF

As you lead your team, your goal should be to help every person get to the place where they are doing their should-dos and love-to-dos, because that is where they will be most effective. As a rule of thumb, try to hire, train, and position people in such a way that 80 percent of the time they work in their strength zone; 15 percent of the time they work in a learning zone; 5 percent of the time they work outside their strength zone; and 0 percent of the time they work in their weakness zone. To facilitate that, you must really know your people, understand their strengths and weaknesses, and be willing to have candid conversations with them. If you've done your work of building strong relationships, then you should be ready, willing, and able to do those things.

Review whether your team members are working in their strength zones. If any are not, what can you do to change that?

DAY

Change is the law of life, and those who look only to the past or present are certain to miss the future.

JOHN F. KENNEDY

Progress always requires change. That's a fact. Most leaders desire to create progress. It's one of the things that make them tick. However, only when leaders reach the level of real productivity are they in a place where they can start to effect change. Why is that? Well, once you've helped the team to achieve some results, you've got the credibility and the momentum to start making changes. It's very difficult to make changes when an organization is standing still. Get it going in any direction and you will find it easier to make changes to move it in the right direction. Momentum provides the energy for needed change. Change in an organization is always a leadership issue. It takes a leader to create positive change. And the best way to start working as a change agent is the same as when trying to build a relationship. You need to find common ground. I'll explain that in tomorrow's reading.

Write down three positive changes your team needs to be making and how you can initiate those changes.

DAY

71

To promote cooperation and teamwork, remember:
People tend to resist that which is forced upon them.
People tend to support that which they help to create.

VINCE PFAFF

Any leader who wants to make changes is tempted to point out differences and try to convince others why change is needed. But that rarely works. Instead, focus on the similarities and build upon those. To get started, look for common ground in the following areas: *Vision*: When the vision is similar, you all see it clearly, and everyone has a strong desire to see it come to fruition, you can probably work well together. *Values*: It's difficult to travel with others very long if your values don't align. *Relationships*: Great teams have people who are as committed to one another as they are to the vision. *Attitude*: If you are going to get people to work together for positive change, their attitudes need to be positive and tenacious. *Communication*: For change to occur, communication must be open, honest, and ongoing. If you can find or create common ground in these five areas, you can move forward and introduce change.

What areas of common ground have you established, and what areas do you need to improve with your team in order to move forward together and make changes?

DAY

72

More men are failures on account of success than on account of failures. They beat their way over a dozen obstacles, overcome a host of difficulties, sacrifice, and sweat. They make the impossible the possible; then along comes a little success, and it tumbles them from their perch. They let up, they slip and over they go.

HENRY FORD

Good leaders keep pushing. If they gain momentum, they don't back off and coast. They press on and increase the momentum so that they can accomplish even greater things. And they help their people do the same. How are they able to stay focused and accomplish so much—despite success as well as failure? Once again Henry Ford has a suggestion. "Make your future plans so long and so hard," Ford advised, "that the people who praise you will always seem to you to be talking about something very trivial in comparison with what you are really trying to do. It is better to have a job too big for popular praise, so big that you can get a good start on it before the cheer squad can get its first intelligent glimmering of your plans. Then you will be free to work and continue your journey toward even greater success."

What can you put into place in your inner life that will help you press on and increase the momentum you are gaining for the long-term future?

DAY

73

You can tell you're on the road to success;
it's uphill all the way.

PAUL HARVEY

Continued growth in leadership isn't easy. It takes effort. It also requires sacrifices. The skills you've developed and used to win today won't necessarily be the ones that you need to win in the future. You'll have to give up some privileges and resources to increase your leadership capacity. You'll have to give up doing some of the things you love that don't give a great enough return on your time. And some people you'd love to take with you will refuse to go. Leaders learn to let go of everything but the essentials as they continue to grow. No leader who ever achieved great things ever said, "It was easier than I thought and took less time." As you work to grow, prepare yourself for the sacrifices you'll have to make to improve as a leader.

Are there sacrifices that you've been putting off that you need to make now to grow as a leader? Write them down and commit yourself to making them.

DAY

74

I start with the premise that the function of leadership is to produce more leaders, not more followers.

RALPH NADER

Leadership is an exciting journey, and leading a productive team is quite an accomplishment. Achieving goals can be very rewarding. But there is more to leadership than just getting work done effectively and adding to the bottom line. What's better than excellence at your work and high productivity from your team? Developing people so that they can lead with you. Great leaders measure themselves by what they get done through others. That requires developing people in a leadership culture. If you have reached the point where you lead a productive team, congratulations. You've achieved more than most people ever do. But don't settle there. Start thinking in terms of how you can help the individuals on your team to improve themselves and tap into their potential.

Have you made the challenging decision to develop your people? Write a declaration of commitment to invest yourself in others' development. Then sign and date it.

DAY

75

*Leadership is unlocking people's
potential to become better.*

BILL BRADLEY

How do you make an organization better? Invest in the people who work in it. Companies get better when their people get better. That's why investing in people always gives a greater return to an organization. Everything rises and falls on leadership. The *more* leaders an organization has, the greater its horsepower. The *better* leaders an organization has, the greater its potential. You cannot overinvest in people. Every time you increase the ability of a person in the organization, you increase the ability to fulfill the vision. Everything gets better when good leaders are leading the organization and creating a positive, productive work environment.

Which team members do you regard as being the keys to helping fulfill the vision for your area? What can you invest in them this week to increase their abilities? Write it down and do it.

DAY

76

If employers fail to upgrade their workers, then they're trying to be competitive only with their capital. Anybody can replicate physical capital. But the one resource nobody can replicate is the dedication, the teamwork, the skills of a company's employees.

ROBERT REICH

People are any organization's most appreciable asset. Good leaders invest their time, energy, money, and thinking into growing others as leaders. They look at every person and try to gauge his or her potential to grow and lead—regardless of the individual's title, position, age, or experience. Every person is a potential candidate for development. This practice of identifying and developing people compounds the positives of the organization, because bringing out the best in a person is often a catalyst for bringing out the best in the team. Developing one person for leadership and success lays the foundation for developing others for success.

Who among your team members shows leadership potential? In what ways?

DAY

77

*The test of your leadership is not what happens when you
are there, but what happens when you're not there.*

KEN BLANCHARD

In my early years of leadership, I left an organization and was disappointed to see that as soon as my personal touch was no longer on a particular task or effort, it wasn't sustained. I had flunked the leadership test! I realized I was doing everything myself, and as long as I ran quickly, I could hold everything together. But the moment I stopped, everything would crash around me. By not training anyone else to help lead, I was wearing myself out and limiting the potential of my organization. What a mistake. That was when I made developing others to lead a priority in my organization. It has revolutionized my leadership and made an incredible impact on every organization I've led. Don't allow yourself to become the lid on your area. Give it the best chance for a bright future by developing other leaders.

Are you doing all the leading yourself as I once did? What steps can you take today to pull others into the process of development to share the responsibilities?

DAY

78

*If your actions inspire others to dream more, learn more,
do more, and become more, you are a leader.*

JOHN QUINCY ADAMS

People development by its very nature shares responsibility for getting things done. I say that because people development is more than just teaching. It's transforming. It invites people into the process of leadership because many things can be learned only through experience. History provides abundant examples of people whose greatest gift was in redeeming, inspiring, liberating, and nurturing the gifts of others. When you give someone responsibility and authority, they not only learn, but they also start to fulfill their leadership responsibilities. That action of empowerment of others to share the leadership load transforms people and organizations.

Who is the person who most inspired and nurtured your development as a leader? What lessons did you learn from that person that you can use in how you develop others?

DAY

One rule of action more important than all others consists in never doing anything that someone else can do for you.

CALVIN COOLIDGE

When you develop people and empower them to lead, their territories expand and so does yours, and it gives you something you can get only by developing others: it gives you back time. You are freed up to do more important things, the most important of which are often thinking, envisioning, and strategizing. You may find it difficult to hand over responsibility for a task to others, especially if you believe they won't do as good a job as you will. But you cannot continue to grow as an effective leader unless you are willing to let go of some of your responsibilities. So what's a good rule of thumb for transferring ownership of a leadership responsibility to someone else? I use the 80 percent rule. If someone on my team can do one of my tasks 80 percent as well as I do (or better), then I give him or her responsibility for it. If you want to be an effective leader, you must move from perfectionist to pragmatist.

What responsibilities are you currently handling that another team member could do 80 percent as well? What steps will you take to hand over that responsibility?

DAY

80

Victory is much more meaningful when it comes not just from one person, but from the joint achievements of many. The euphoria is lasting when all participants lead with their hearts, winning not just for themselves but for one another.

HOWARD SCHULTZ

The greatest satisfaction and the richest experiences in life come from giving to others. We are most fulfilled when we forget ourselves and focus on others. Rabbi Harold Kushner asserted, "The purpose of life is not to win. The purpose of life is to grow and to share. When you come to look back on all that you have done in life, you will get more satisfaction from the pleasures you have brought into other people's lives than you will from the times that you outdid and defeated them." That is great wisdom. Helping others grow and develop brings great joy, satisfaction, and energy to a leader. If you can be a developer of other people, you will create a sense of community where victories are celebrated, gratitude is evident, and loyalty is shared.

Take the time to honestly review your attitude toward the development of other team members. Write down your thoughts. Is your heart really in it? If not, why not?

DAY

81

If you get the best players and coach them
soundly, you're going to win.

BOBBY BOWDEN

Recruiting is the first and most important task in developing people and creating winning organizations. You can't develop people without potential—no matter how hard you work at it. So the people you recruit must possess natural ability in the area where they are to be developed, exhibit the desire to grow, and be a good fit for the organization. That requires having the right chemistry. If you are seriously considering recruiting or promoting someone, keep in mind that if you don't like the person, you will not be an effective mentor to them. It's very difficult to spend time with people, be open with them, and invest in them if you don't like them or want to be around them. Also ask members of your team to spend time with that individual, in a social setting if possible. After they've been around the person, find out if your team likes and would enjoy working with him or her. If not, there may not be a good fit.

Previously you identified individuals from your team whom you feel have the greatest potential to lead and make an impact. Do they have the right chemistry with you and other members of your team?

DAY

82

Good people are found,
not changed.

JIM ROHN

When I look for potential leaders, along with chemistry I consider a candidate's character. Good character makes trust possible. Trust makes strong relationships possible. Strong relationships make mentoring possible. You won't be able to develop someone whose character you do not trust. Character is what closes the gap between knowing and doing. It aligns intentions and action. That consistency is appealing, and it is also essential to good, credible leadership. If I suspect that someone I'm considering recruiting doesn't have strong character, I don't go through with it. If you go into a mentoring relationship expecting to change a person's character, you're liable to be disappointed.

From among the potential leaders you've identified from your team, describe the quality of their characters. What gives you the confidence to trust them?

DAY

83

*The stars can at any time meet
the requirements needed to help the team.
Support players can sometimes do that.*

CHARLES BARKLEY

As you look at potential leaders to develop, you must not ask for what they wish they could give, only for what they have the potential to give. To bring out the best in people, you need to assess their capacity for leadership in the following areas:

○ *Stress Management*—their ability to withstand and overcome pressure, failure, deadlines, and obstacles.
○ *Skill*—their ability to get specific tasks done.
○ *Thinking*—their ability to be creative, develop strategy, solve problems, and adapt.
○ *Leadership*—their ability to gather followers and build a team.
○ *Attitude*—their ability to remain positive and tenacious amidst negative circumstances.

As a leader, your goal should be to identify what their capacity is, recognize what *they* think their capacity is, and motivate, challenge, and equip them in such a way that they close the gap between the two.

Referring to the five areas I have listed, how do you assess the leadership capacity of the team members whom you feel have the potential to lead? Write a review of each of them carefully and honestly.

DAY

84

I've had good players and I've had bad players.
I'm a better coach with good players.

LOU HOLTZ

If you want to develop better leaders, I've suggested you recruit people with potential according to chemistry, character, and capacity. Add one other "C" quality to that list: contribution. Some people possess an X factor. They are winners. They contribute beyond their job responsibilities, and they lift the performance of everyone on their team. When you discover people with these characteristics, recruit them. They are a joy to develop, and whatever you put into them returns to you compounded. If you want to be better, recruit better people. If you want to develop better leaders, recruit people with potential according to the Four C's.

Who among the potential leaders on your team stands out for their contribution? Describe their contributions. These are the people to target for development.

....

....

....

....

....

....

....

....

....

....

....

....

....

....

....

....

....

....

....

....

DAY

85

*The secret is to work less as individuals
and more as a team. As a coach, I play not my eleven best,
but my best eleven.*

KNUTE ROCKNE

Championship team coaches realize that it's not enough just to recruit good players. A leader must understand how those players best fit on the team and put them there. To do that, he must have a clear picture of each person's strengths and weaknesses and understand how they fit the needs of the team. In his book *Good to Great*, Jim Collins writes about this principle: the importance of getting the right people in the right seats on the bus. Successful people find their right seats. Successful leaders help their people find their right seats. Sometimes that requires moving people around to find where they make the greatest contribution. Sometimes it means trying and failing. As a leader, you have to take it all in stride. Positioning people correctly is a process, and you have to treat it that way. But if you don't do it, you will never help your people reach their potential.

As you've considered your team members, do you feel that any of them should be repositioned? What process will you put into place to make that happen?

DAY

86

*The best example of leadership
is leadership by example.*
JERRY MCCAIN

While I've already written about how important it is to model what you want to see in others, here are the things I believe I must model with integrity in order to help people to develop into leaders.

- *Authenticity*—This is the foundation for developing people.
- *Servanthood*—This is the soul for developing people.
- *Growth*—This is the measurement for developing people.
- *Excellence*—This is the standard for developing people.
- *Passion*—This is the fuel for developing people.
- *Success*—This is the purpose for developing people.

It is impossible to help others grow if your life does not model what they need to become.

When your team members watch you lead, what do you think they see that makes them want to develop their own potential? In what ways do you need to improve and grow?

DAY

87

The largest single source of failed promotion is the failure to think through and help others to think through what a new job requires.

PETER DRUCKER

It's not enough to simply tell people what they need to do. That's not developing their potential. Instead, a leader must help them to do their jobs and do them well. How does a leader equip people to do their work and succeed at it? The best method I've found is a five-step equipping process. Here's how it works:

- ○ Step 1—I do it (competence).
- ○ Step 2—I do it and you are with me (demonstration).
- ○ Step 3—You do it and I am with you (coaching).
- ○ Step 4—You do it (empowerment).
- ○ Step 5—You do it and someone is with you (reproduction).

If you adopt this method, not only will you equip leaders, you will begin teaching them how to equip others, which sets them up to become leaders who develop others.

Write down one task you will demonstrate to one of your team members today with the intention that you will equip and empower them to accomplish this task independently in the future.

DAY

*The individual leads in order that those who
are led can develop their potential as human beings
and thereby prosper.*

SOCRATES

If the only thing you're helping a new leader learn is how to get ahead in the workplace, you're not truly developing that person to succeed, because there's a lot more to life than work and career. It is the responsibility of a leader in the development of other leaders to help people to learn how to do life well. A good leader is always on the lookout for a person's weaknesses and wrong thinking—not to exploit that person, but to strengthen and help him or her succeed. Then the leader will challenge them in every area of their lives where you see that they need improvement. And beyond the challenge, a good leader is there to help and support them through the process and to help new leaders navigate through life's difficulties.

Is there someone you work with who has the skill and desire to do well, yet constantly seems to struggle? Why do you think that is? Is there some advice you can give that person in an encouraging manner?

DAY

89

The best executive is the one who has sense enough to pick good men to do what he wants done, and self-restraint enough to keep from meddling with them while they do it.

THEODORE ROOSEVELT

I have to admit that as a leader, it's hard not to meddle. That's especially true when you know the work you're delegating very well, but the person to whom you're giving it is new to it. Yet releasing work to be done by others is an essential link to empowering and ultimately developing them as leaders. As you delegate tasks to the leaders you're developing, you need to trust them, believe in them, and hold them accountable. When you trust another person, that trust creates a bond between you and them. When you believe in people, you motivate them. Few things put wind in another person's sails like your faith in them. And the belief must be genuine. Pretending you believe provides no passion for empowerment. And when you hold people accountable, you increase their chances for positive results. Why? Because everyone finds focus in goals. They work better toward deadlines. And they usually rise to the level of a leader's expectations. Without accountability, people drift. With it, they achieve results.

Write down three tasks that you will release to team members whom you are developing and record how you will hold them accountable for the results.

DAY

90

The final test of a leader is that he leaves behind him in other men the convictions and the will to carry on.

WALTER LIPPMANN

Regardless of where you are in your leadership journey, I want to give you a vision of what some leaders achieve—what I call the Pinnacle of leadership. These rare individuals lead so well for so long that they create a legacy of leadership in the organization they serve. Pinnacle leaders stand out from everyone else. Leaders at the pinnacle of their leadership have guided other leaders to the point that they in turn are developing new leaders. They are a cut above, and they seem to bring success with them wherever they go. Leadership at this high level lifts the entire organization and creates an environment that benefits everyone in it, contributing to their success. Pinnacle leaders often possess an influence that transcends the organization and the industry the leader works in.

Few people reach the Pinnacle, but all leaders leave a legacy. What do you hope your legacy will be?

Look for the next book in the JumpStart series

Learn how to maximize your potential with this 90-day improvement plan, based on the #1 *New York Times* bestseller *The 15 Invaluable Laws of Growth.* Maxwell delivers daily inspiration and practical advice for bringing out your best, personally and professionally, one day at a time. Including engaging lessons, thought-provoking questions, inspiring quotes, and journaling space to track your progress, this portable guide offers everything you need to experience personal growth in just three short months.

Coming in 2015 from Center Street
wherever books are sold.

CENTER
STREET

NEW YORK · BOSTON · NASHVILLE

Introducing the JumpStart Series Community on Facebook

Find other fans of the JumpStart series and maximize your personal and professional growth.

- ⚉ Interact with other like-minded leaders.
- ⚉ Receive and share inspiring quotes with your friends.
- ⚉ Engage with thought-provoking questions and answers.
- ⚉ Get the latest news about upcoming books in the JumpStart series and receive exclusive information.
- ⚉ Experience a daily community where you can get ideas on how to apply what you learn.

Visit www.facebook.com/TheJumpStartSeries
and Like the page to get started.